# PAWS
## at
# WORK

## A Service Dog and Her Veteran

Mary Hahn Ward

First Edition

MHW Creative Works, Wilmington, NC

Paws at Work
     By Mary Hahn Ward

Published by:
MHW Creative Works
Wilmington, NC

www.maryhahnward.com

All photographs by: Mary Hahn Ward
Edits by: Kate Ward
Interior Design by: AmyLee Pettis
Front and Back Covers Design by: AmyLee Pettis

ISBN-10: 0692729607
ISBN-13: 978-0692729601

First Edition

# DEDICATION

This book is dedicated to Patriot Paws, and Lori Stevens, the founder. Lori, and all of those that work with her, are the reason precious dogs such as Maddie are available to people with disabilities. Visit http://www.patriotpaws.org to find out more about the program and how you might be able to help.

"In *Paws at Work* we learn that heroes come in all shapes and sizes - some are former Marines in wheelchairs and others are yellow haired angels on four paws. An important read for all ages that helps explain the dedication that goes into caring for our nation's heroes, and the vital, and often misunderstood role that service animals play. The beautiful photography offers a peek into their daily life together and lets the love between Tom and Maddie shine through."

*~ Sarah Verardo*

"Reading and sharing *Paws at Work* is a remarkable opportunity. Children, teachers and parents will all learn from Tom and Maddie's adventures together, but will also be moved by the relationship between this remarkable dog and her veteran. Mary Hahn Ward's loving photographs add a visceral sense of realism to the relationship -- both its challenges and its wonders. Bravo, Maddie!"

*~ Deavours Hall, PhD,*
*Writer with a special interest in social justice and education*

"Mary Hahn Ward's *Paws at Work: A Service Dog and her Veteran* shows the work of a fabulous service dog named Maddie. Mary draws the reader in to the story through Maddie's voice as she describes her life and daily duties. "Paws at Work" is an entertaining narrative that not only documents the life of Maddie and her handler but also educates the reader about the importance of service dogs. The end of the book lists brief reminders to the reader. This list provides quick and useful information to any person who may come into contact with a service dog and their handler. "Paws at Work: A Service Dog and Her Veteran" is a great resource to the service dog community."

*~ Larkin Rogers, 2nd grade teacher, Charlotte, NC*

# ACKNOWLEDGMENTS

Thank you Patriot Paws trainers, volunteers, and donors. This story could not be told without all of those who had a role in training Maddie. Nor could it be told without the cooperation and interest of Tom Ward, Maddie's handler, and the love of her life. The nuts and bolts of writing and editing were only possible with the assistance of Kate Ward. I am eternally thankful that she finds it easy to tell me what doesn't work so that we can figure out what does. My designer, AmyLee Pettis, said yes to taking this on before I finished asking the question. As much beauty as the look and feel has to the book it pales next to AmyLee's heart. She is a veteran who has served her country well. AmyLee cares for her veteran husband and is a dedicated mom to her two girls. Jennifer Mackinday, I can't thank her enough for encouraging me to be bold with this project. When I asked if Jennifer would help with marketing and public relations she said yes and hit the ground running. Jennifer is a caregiver for her brother, a wounded warrior, and the mom of a son who serves as a Marine. I am deeply grateful to all of you.

Special thank you to Koolway Sports, and in particular, Jennifer Gallienne and John Cook for their extraordinary creativity, and passion, to help people who rely on wheelchairs for mobility to be warm outdoors while maintaining their Koolness with this innovative outerwear. Go to page 13 to see the Koolway jacket and blanket on Tom. It is the most wonderful piece of warm weather gear he has ever owned. Please visit the website for more information: http://koolwaysports.com.

A very special thank you to Shannon Allen for her vision, and dedication, to assist wounded warriors and disabled veterans requiring the assistance of a wheelchair for mobility in funding Koolway outwear that suits them. Shannon struggled to find a coat that would work for her husband who was catastrophically wounded while serving in Afghanistan. We can't thank Shannon, and her organization KBW3, enough for granting Tom his Kooyway outwear. To find out more about Shannon, her husband, and KBW3 please visit the website: http://www.warriorallianceproject.org/kbw3.

Maddie is a Yellow Labrador Retriever. She is a special dog, a service dog. When she was five weeks old she started training. It took two years of training for her to be ready to help a person with disabilities.

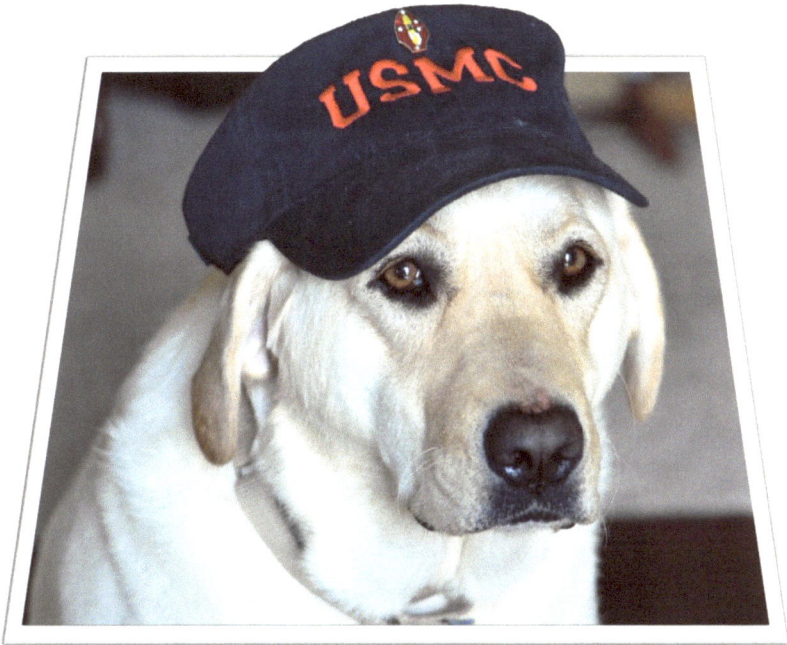

"This is the best job a dog can have. I love my work!" says Maddie.

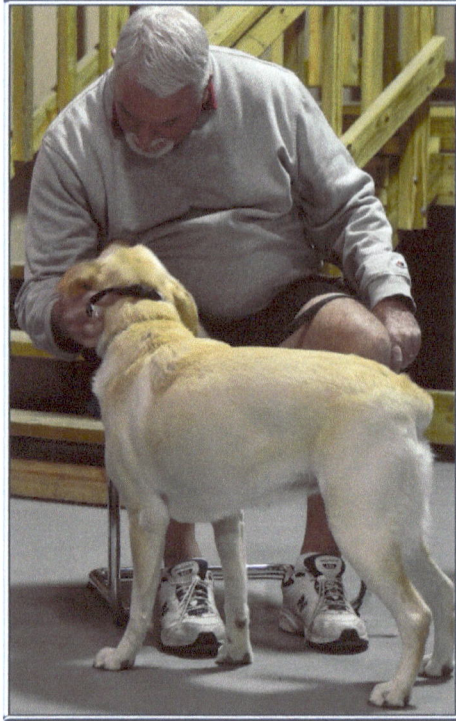

On this day Maddie was awarded to Tom. It was also her birthday. She turned two years old! Maddie remembers, "We had a party celebrating my birthday. Tom bought the dogs a dog cake and the people a delicious chocolate cake!"

Tom is a U.S. Marine Corps veteran. He has disabilities caused by a disease that makes his muscles stop working. The disease has a big name: Amyotrophic Lateral Sclerosis so, instead, people say ALS.

"I'm looking forward to helping him. I know I will have a positive impact on his life!"

Maddie was trained in Texas. Tom traveled to Texas so they could work together for her last two weeks of training. On the last day of training Maddie graduates and is ready for her life of service with Tom!

It was a big day when Tom and Maddie went home together for the first time. Tom was a little nervous. They had to travel on an airplane to get there because he lives more than a thousand miles away in North Carolina.

Maddie was not worried at all. She was trained to ride on buses, trains, airplanes, and in cars.

"I've got this. I'm not nervous at all. I'm a really good traveler and I love airplanes. I'll help him every step of the way." And she did.

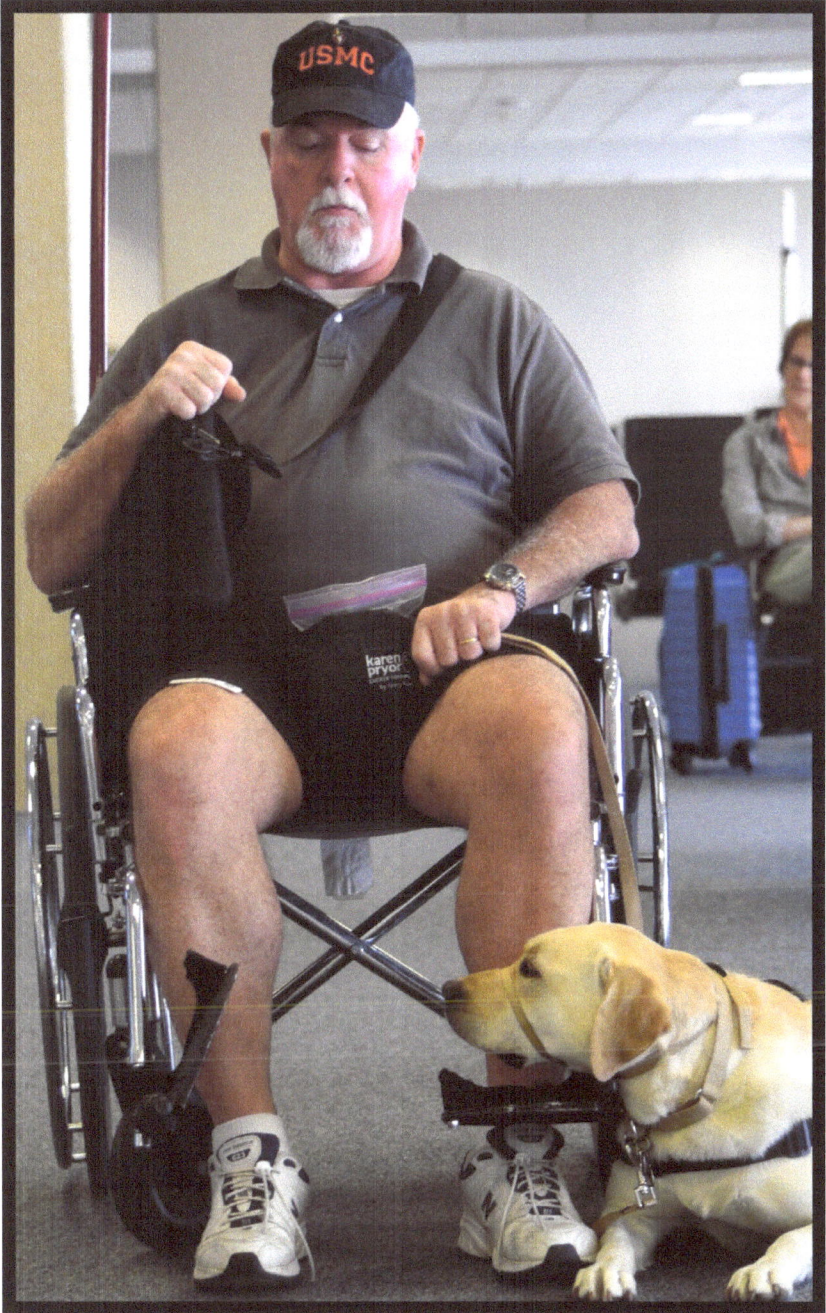

Maddie wears a vest when she is busy working. She likes it! Her vest says, *Working Dog Do Not Pet*. This is an important message.

Maddie wants you to know how she feels, "I want to concentrate on taking care of Tom. If everyone interacts with me when we are out I might forget to help him and he could get hurt. It might cause me to pull on the leash and that would affect his balance, leading to a fall!"

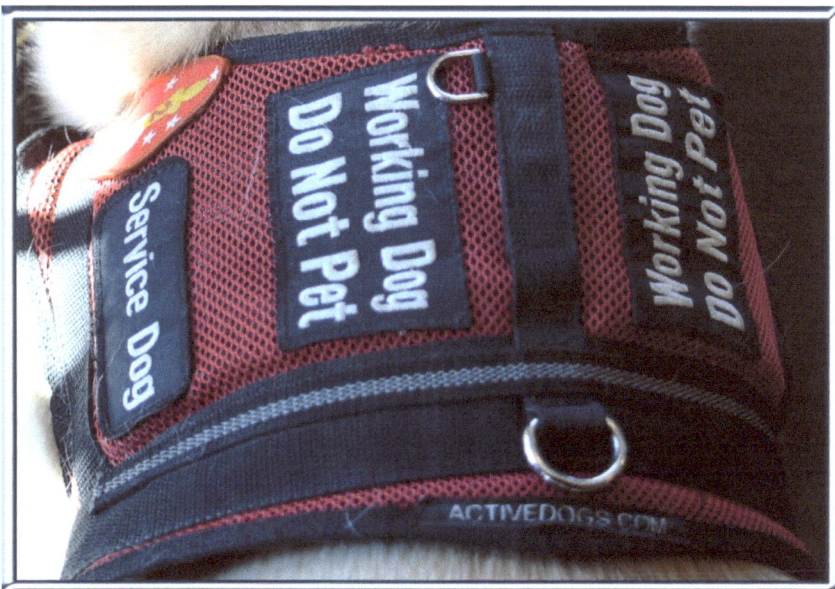

It is important for a service dog and their handler to bond. A handler is the person the service dog cares for every day just like a handler might use a cane or a wheelchair. A service dog is an important tool for the handler's mobility, only better, because they have fur and hearts. Their bond will help them be a good team!

"Sometimes Tom says 'see me' and we look into each other's eyes. When I do it right I get a treat! I love Tom so much!!"

Tom and Maddie often go out in public. They go to museums, shopping, the beach, restaurants and many other places. When Tom goes out to eat Maddie is never distracted by the delicious smells coming from the kitchen or from the food on the table above her head. She mostly goes under tables when they are out to eat but sometimes she will lie beside them.

"Tom gives me the cue 'under' when I am going under a table while he eats. Most of the time I like it under there but sometimes it is a little tight for me so he lets me lay along side the table. Either way I am quiet and still for the whole time he is dining. I don't eat anything that drops on the floor because it could make me sick. Tom reminds me to 'leave it' if it looks like I might be interested in it. I lay close to him so if Tom drops his napkin or fork I pick it up for him because his fingers do not work well anymore."

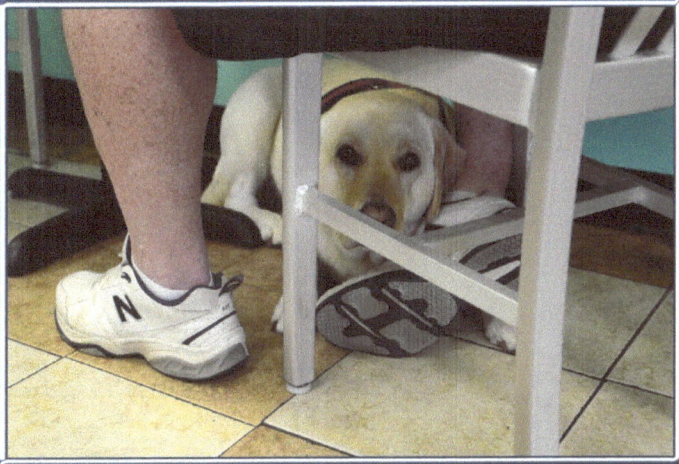

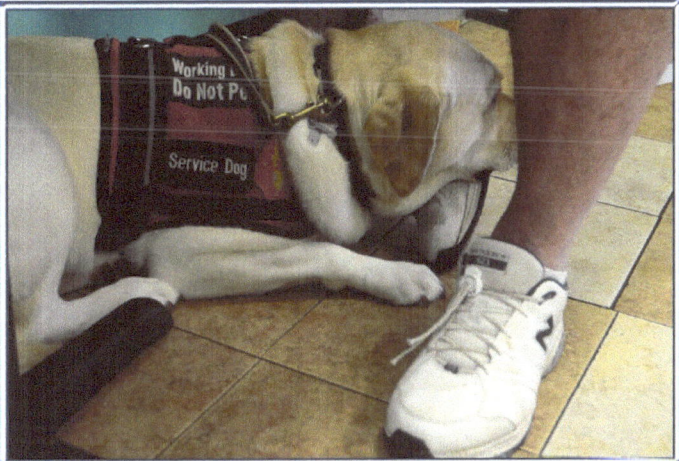

Since Tom has had ALS he feels the cold more than he use to. He says he feels it right down to his bones. He has a custom made jacket that zips up to a custom made blanket that is like a sleeping bag. The jacket and blanket are fleece lined. It is so warm that he can take his shoes and socks off when he is wearing it. Maddie likes it too. She is tuned into him to the point where she knows if he is uncomfortable, tired, hurt, or weaker.

"When it is cold outside and Tom is in his wheelchair I take good care of him. I make sure his legs are covered up. Blankets used to get caught in his wheels. His new blanket is like a sleeping bag, it's awesome. It is efficient and tidy!"

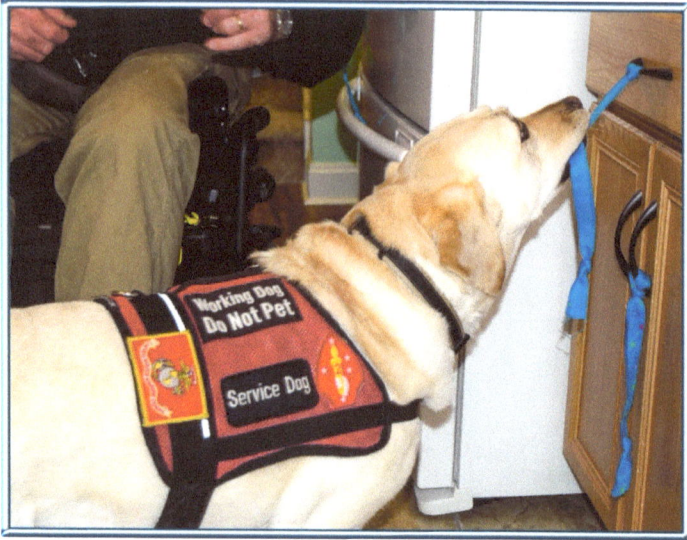

Maddie is a true asset in the kitchen. To open a drawer, or door, she pulls on a piece of cord. Tom asks her to "pull" for this job. After he gets what he needs he asks her to "push" and she closes them with the tip of her nose.

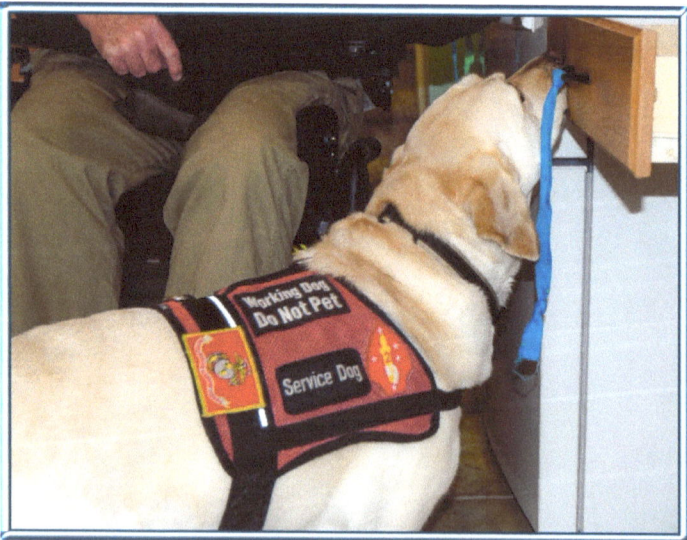

Maddie's strength and agility is evident when she opens and closes the refrigerator door. Tom gives the same cue, "pull," to open it, but to close the door he says "up." Maddie gets up on her hind legs and pushes the door closed with her front legs. It is remarkable how smoothly she does this task.

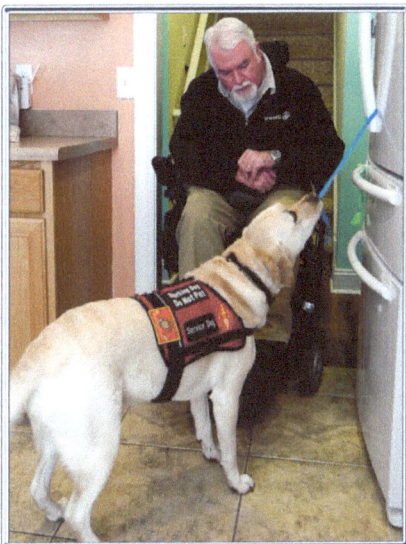

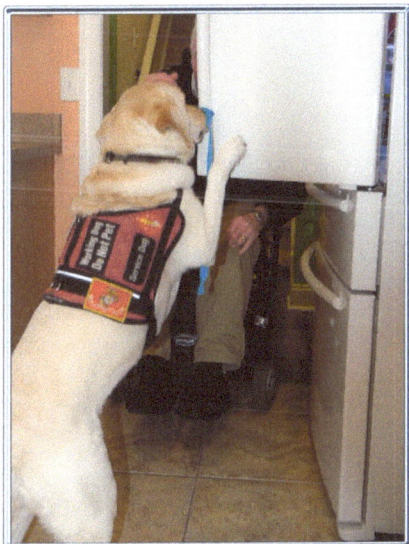

"I get great joy out of closing the door. It is fun to get up on my back legs and use my front ones to push the door. It is almost like jumping when I am outside playing!"

The muscles in Tom's hands and fingers make picking up dropped items difficult. When Tom says "uh-oh," Maddie will get the objects from the floor and give them to him.

"Learning to pick up stuff off the floor and giving it to someone was difficult. I have to use my incisors in the front of my mouth to pick it up and hold on to it. Then I drop it in someone's hand. Sometimes I get rewarded with a little treat or some affection. I like it best when I get both!"

Service dogs are permitted everywhere, even doctors' offices. The exceptions are when a sterile environment must be maintained. Tom and Maddie go many places together. One of their favorite trips has been to Washington, D.C.

"Even though it is a lot of work for me I like when we travel. It is a lot of work because it usually means more walking for me. It means lots of stimulation that I am not used to, which I ignore pretty well EXCEPT for the smells of lots of other dogs. I love those smells!"

For Tom to travel anywhere he must have a wheelchair accessible van with a ramp. The ramp allows him to take his wheelchair. Maddie travels in the van with him. He tells her to "load up" when it is time to get in the van. When they get to where they are going and it is time for Maddie to get out, he says "let's go."

"I'm pretty smart. When Tom turns on his power wheelchair it makes a beeping sound. Every time I hear it, I get ready. He hardly ever gets to finish saying 'let's go' because I know just what to do!

"Sometimes it is a tight fit getting out of the van. Tom tells me 'back' so I don't get squished between the van seat and his wheelchair. As he starts to move forward he asks me to 'follow' and off we go to another adventure."

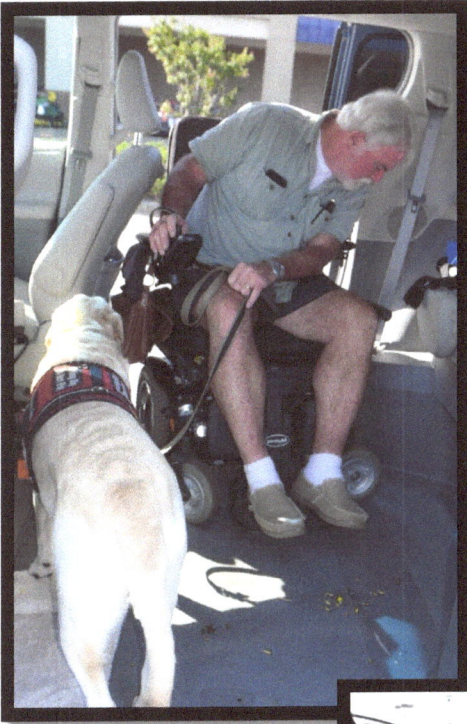

One of Tom's favorite places to shop is the hardware store. He likes tools and figuring out how to adapt them to his abilities. Maddie patiently goes along with him. When he stops to look at something he tells her to "halt" and she quietly sits next to him.

"Tom can take as long he needs to when we are out and about. I'm just happy to be with him. However, it's not so much fun when people try to talk to me or pet me. It happens a lot when we are in public places. It confuses me when they do this and makes me work even harder to pay attention to Tom. I can tell some people think Tom is mean when he tells them they can't talk to me or know my name or pet me. He is helping me to stay on task, just like I help him. We are a team of two."

A special place for Tom is the beach. He enjoys the magnificence of the ocean, the sound of the waves, the beautifully expansive sky, and the smell of salt water. As the ALS takes more of his ability to walk from him it doesn't stop him from going to the beach. There are boardwalks that accommodate his power wheelchair and Maddie.

"It is true about dogs and their acute sense of smell. It's a challenge for me to stay focused when we are at the beach. There must be a thousand different smells coming at me from all directions. I try really hard to stay focused on Tom, but sometimes I just can't help it. I have to smell the beach smells!"

When Tom's legs were stronger, he set his easel up on the beach in the sand and painted beach scenes. Even though being in the sand is not an option for Tom anymore, it doesn't stop him from painting at the beach. He paints on the boardwalk with his wheelchair close to him in case he needs to give his legs a rest. With paintbrush in hand, he loses himself in these creative moments. He forgets he has ALS. He becomes, very much, in the moment.

"Sometimes I feel bad for Tom. Every time we go to the beach he lays down a blanket for me. I'm not sure why. Maybe he wants me to be free of sand or he thinks it's more comfortable for me. To make him feel good I lay on the blanket, for like a second. As soon as he starts painting and sort of forgets about me, I scoot off the blanket and squish into the sand...smelling, smelling, smelling. Sometimes a little bird comes close to me, taunts me by hopping around, but I never give chase. I stay just where I am so Tom can keep painting and not worry about me."

When Maddie talks to Tom, she makes chuffing, grunting sounds. Tom usually starts the conversation off by getting real close to her face. Before you know it she's talking his ear off. She has a lot to say most days.

"If Tom could understand dog language he would laugh when I was talking to him. I'm usually trying to convince him that we should go play with the ball. I come up with great reasons why throwing the ball for me is important, but since he doesn't know what I'm saying, it goes in one ear and out the other!"

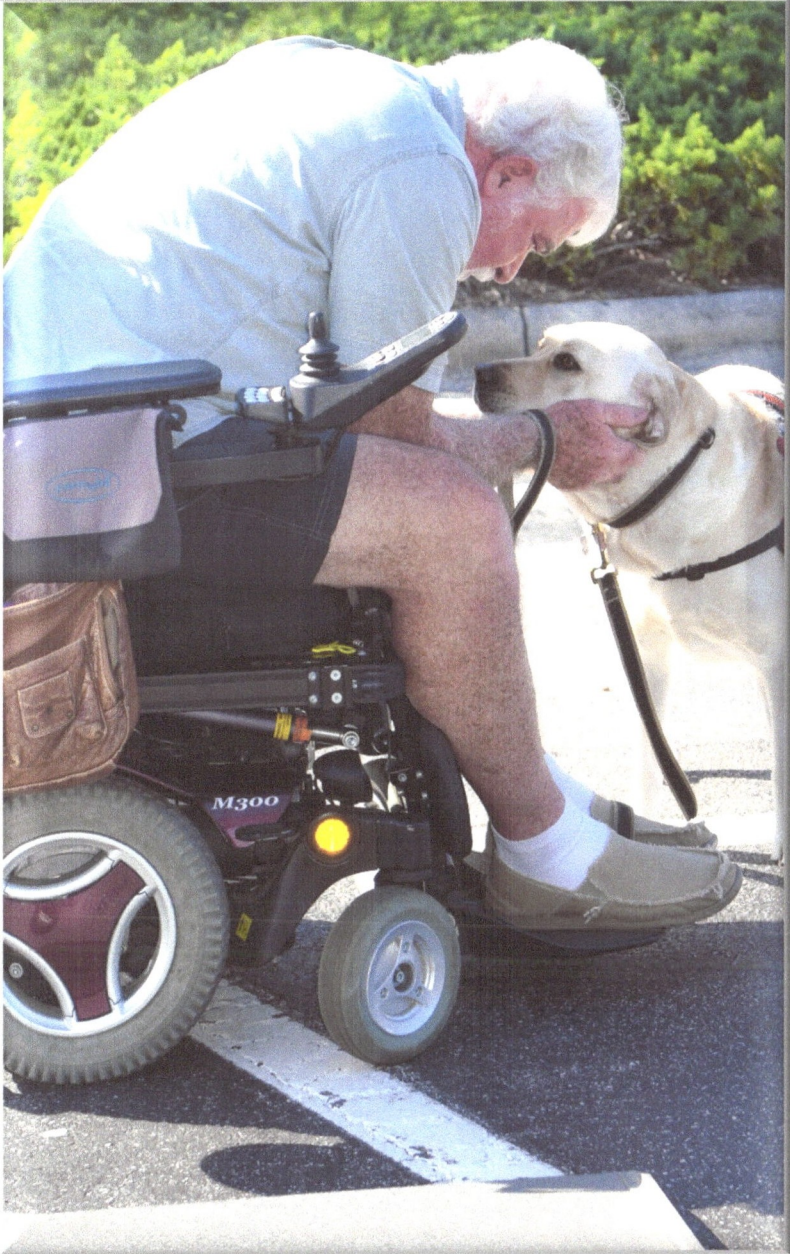

Maddie has a perfect disposition to be a service dog. She is gentle and submissive. She has a kind look to her. Maddie is a true beauty inside and out.

"My beauty works for and against me. It works for me because what girl doesn't want to be beautiful? It works against me when people want to pet and talk to me because they love how I look. I'm eye candy for the public. Fortunately, my training kicks in and I ignore people most of the time. I feel sorry for Tom when people pull out their phones to show him photos of their *beautiful* dogs, especially if he is eating a delicious sandwich and they are interrupting. It's kind of boring when people do that."

Food is synonymous with Labrador Retrievers. Tell Maddie it is snack time and she'll do just about anything - including bring her own napkin to the table!

"Eating is one of my favorite things to do. I love it as much as playing ball. I'm lucky because I was trained with food as a reward. I never stop training, not really. Tom drills me almost every day using food to help me remember what to do. As much as I'd like to say I do every cue perfectly, that would be a lie. He never tells me I'm bad or yells at me when I get it wrong. He ignores it when I do not do something correctly. He redirects me to something really easy like 'touch.' Touch means I touch my nose to his hand and this resets me so I'm ready for a more challenging cue."

Tom likes to give her a little treat in the late afternoon. Tom knows that apples are one of her favorites. His wife peels the apple for Maddie and Tom feeds it to her. She eats it like we eat corn on the cob!

"Apples are so good I would eat the core and the seeds if I could. Tom makes sure I eat just the meat of the apple so that I do not get a bellyache. This is Tom looking out for me again just like I do for him!"

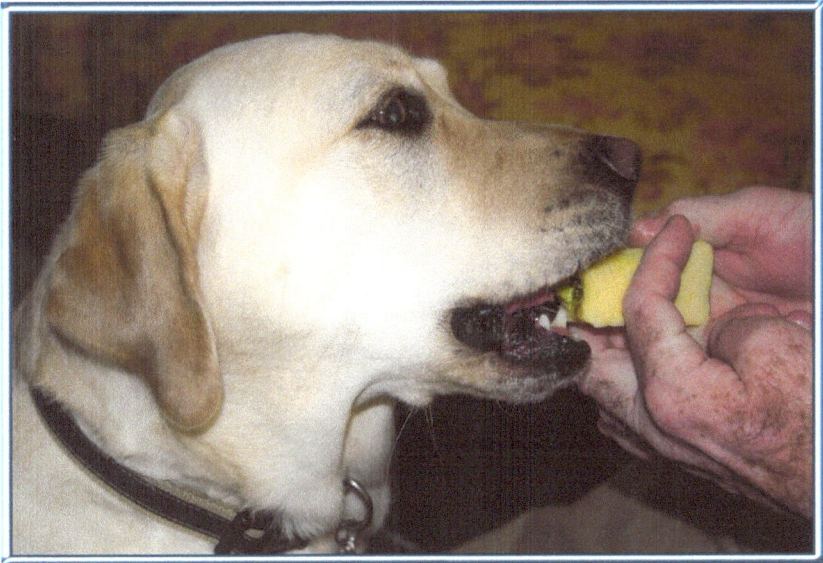

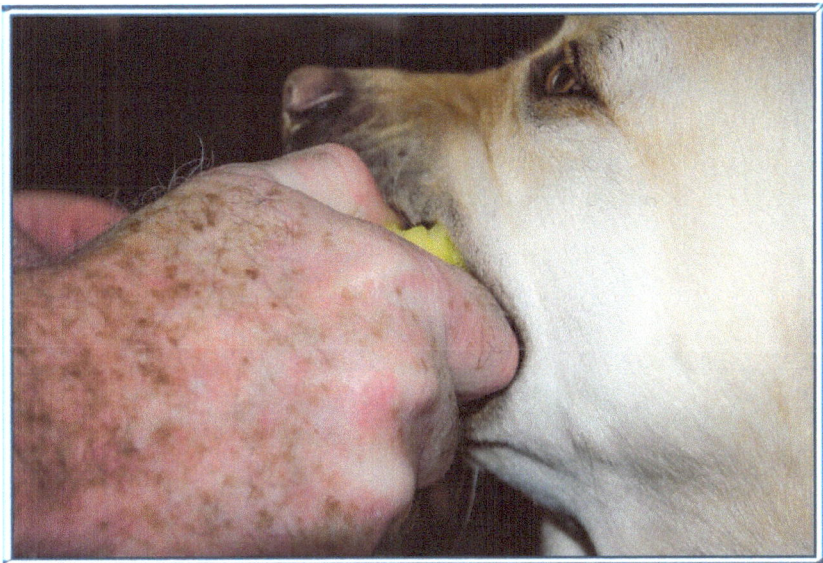

Toward the end of the day, Tom takes Maddie to the backyard to play ball. It is a good reward for all of the work she does during the day. He gets comfortable in a chair so that he doesn't tire out too soon. Tom knows how important play is for Maddie. It gives her a good balance to her day.

"Wow, what can I say about playing ball? It is beyond fun. Tom throws the ball long and I try to get under it to catch it as it is coming down. He throws it so it bounces and I leap in the air for it. Honestly, I'm a spectacular athlete. I could play outfield for a major league team. I'm that good."

"I chase down the ball if it gets out in front of me.

"I catch it in mid-air.
I catch it on a bounce.

"I am on it when it comes to playing ball. I even bring it back and drop it into Tom's hands. 'Give' is a great cue 'cause I know just what he means when he says it. He often drops the ball after I give it to him, but I don't care. I do it again for him! The ALS has affected his hands, so holding on to things like the ball give him trouble. That's why I am so good for him. I help him all the time. I even help him play ball with me! We are amazing together!"

Running fast is part of playing ball and getting some energy out. When Tom is not feeling so strong he and Maddie spend most of the day at home not moving around much. Tom always makes sure she gets in some exercise with ball play on those kind of days!

"Sometimes I get real low to the ground like I'm sneaking up on the ball!"

Play includes rest periods. Tom doesn't want Maddie to get too hot. When he feels she needs to take a break he lets her keep the ball with her in the down position.

"If I could I'd have a ball with me everywhere I go. It makes me happy and satisfied when I get to play like this."

Service dogs should always look their best. Every two to three weeks Tom gives Maddie a bath. She lies on the floor in many public places. Some of those places are not the cleanest.

"I kind of like a bath, but the tub isn't big enough to swim in. I like pushing the water around with my nose. If Tom had a pool I would enjoy that. I definitely do not like to swim in the ocean. It kind of scares me. When it comes down to it a bath is the closest I get to swimming.

"When the washing of me is all done I give a *really, really* BIG shake. My hair gets super wet. It takes a long time to dry. I especially love it when Tom combs my hair. He gets buckets of hair out. We could make another dog with all the hair that comes out! Baths exhausts both of us. However, it's worth it because my coat looks spectacular when it's all over!"

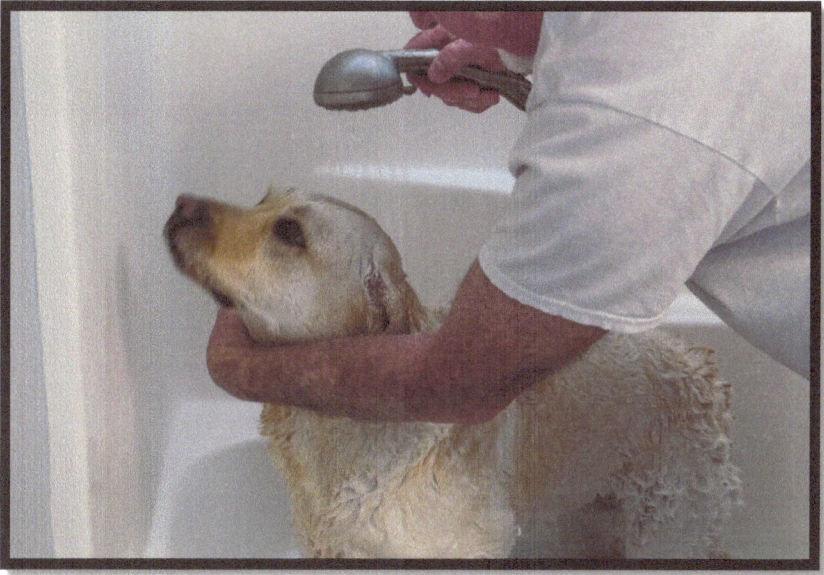

Tom and Maddie have been paired for more than three years. Each day their bond grows stronger. Sometimes when they are sitting quietly she surprises him with some kisses.

"Giving kisses is the best way to show my affection to Tom!"

They are together most of the time, but sometimes he doesn't take her. When he is going to leave a room by himself he gives Maddie the cue "place." He has a special bed just for her that is her place. For almost the entire time he is gone, whether it is a few seconds or a few minutes, she watches for him.

"I'd rather go with Tom. I worry about him when he leaves without me. Suppose he falls or drops something? I won't be close enough to help him. I keep a good lookout for him so I am ready when he returns. If he doesn't come back in a few minutes I kind of forget that he left the room and take a good nap for myself!"

Opening a door while in a wheelchair is a challenge. When Tom and Maddie go shopping if the door is not an automatic one he has to figure out how to open it. If there is a button that can be pushed to make the door open Maddie can do it for him. He cues her with the word "up" and just like when she closes the refrigerator, she gets up on her hind legs to get the job done.

Opening the door with an automatic button is a multi-operational endeavor. Tom pulls his wheelchair in front of the button and cues Maddie to get up so her nose can press it. As the door opens he moves himself and Maddie through the door before it closes. As nice as it is when people want to help, it's easier for them to go through without help. Any distractions can cause Maddie, or Tom, to get hurt by getting stuck in a door that is closing.

"Just like learning to pick up items with my teeth, getting up to press a button to open a door was a difficult task to master. It is still a pretty big deal when I have to do it. We only have seconds from the time Tom tells me 'up' to move from that position and through the door. As Tom gets ready to give me my cues, I anticipate what is coming and have to think about it for a second or two to get ready. Sometimes I stick out my tongue when I know I have a challenge ahead of me."

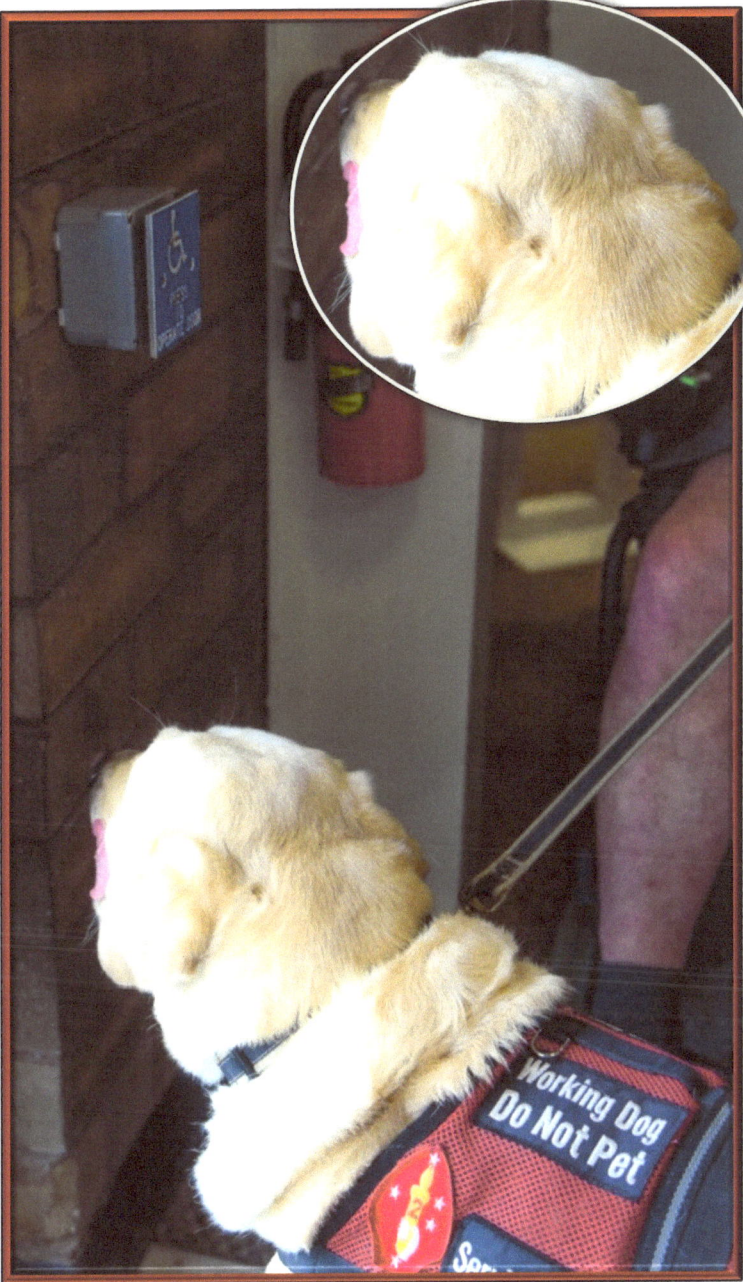

At the end of the day Tom and Maddie often wind down in their backyard. He likes to sit on a bench in the garden and draw on his sketchpad. Maddie gets a chance to hang out without her vest on. She likes lying on the grass, not too far from Tom, but far enough that she has her own space. They enjoy the peace and quiet together.

Tom and Maddie thank you for taking the time to read their story and how they work together. Maddie provides an important service for Tom. She has helped him maintain some independence just a little bit longer than he otherwise would.

Videos of Maddie working and playing: https://goo.gl/VQgruS

Thank You!

When you see someone with a service dog:

Please be respectful to the service dog team and treat them with dignity.

Please let the dog work free of distraction. For example, avoid talking to the dog or reaching in to pet the dog.

Some handlers are not agreeable to allowing anyone to pet or interact with their dog and some are okay with it. Please do not be offended if you are told **no** if you ask to pet the dog.

Some handlers do not mind talking about their service dog when people ask them questions and some handlers prefer to be left alone.

Sometimes it takes a lot of effort for the handler to be out in public to take care of errands and they do not want to talk to others about the dog.
Please do not ask the handler to have the service dog demonstrate tasks. The service dog is trained to assist the handler with their specific needs, not to do "tricks."

Please do not offer food to a service dog. Only the handler decides when and what the service dog can eat. They are trained not to eat off the floor as well as not be a nuisance in a restaurant or supermarket.

Please do not ask a handler what their disability is. It is a private matter.

Children seem to be more educated about service dogs than adults. When encountering a service dog team be more like children and give the team personal space to do their work without interference.

A service dog team is beautiful to watch in action. Instead of trying to be involved with them, stand back and admire their effort.

# ABOUT THE AUTHOR

Mary Hahn Ward is the author of *Letters Home. Paws at Work* is her second book. She holds a graduate degree in Health Services Management and Policy and a Master of Public Administration. She is currently an educator. Mary is the proud mom of a daughter who is an elementary school teacher, a son who is serving the U.S. Army, and is a grandma to a delightful grandson. She is a caregiver to her husband of 36 plus years. Her husband is a U.S. Marine Corps veteran with Amyotrophic Lateral Sclerosis, ALS. Mary is currently serving as a fellow with the Elizabeth Dole Foundation. She advocates on behalf of military/veteran caregivers, and, in particular, those caregivers whose veterans are battling ALS. Mary believes strongly in caregivers taking good care of their mental, and physical health. Her self-care is photography and writing.

www.ingramcontent.com/pod-product-compliance
Lightning Source LLC
LaVergne TN
LVHW010022070426
835508LV00001B/2